Picking up the Pieces: A Mother's Story of How Juvenile Diabetes Affected Her Life

Lori Dotson

ISBN-10: 0615560083
ISBN-13: 978-0615560083

CONTENTS

PREFACE

Written from the perspective of the mother of a child recently diagnosed with juvenile (type 1) diabetes, this true story aims to raise awareness, to educate, and to hopefully, in the end, inspire others who face similar challenges. It describes our experiences and struggles with my daughter Kaitlin's diabetes, as well as my own personal feelings of guilt and helplessness and how my daughter's disease changed my life in the 3 years following her diagnosis.

Type 1 diabetes is the lesser known type, affecting only 5 to 10% of those diagnosed as diabetic. Still, it affects as many as three million Americans, and more than 15,000 children are diagnosed with a new case of type 1 diabetes each year in the U.S. Regretfully, statistics show the rate of increase is on the rise. Type 1 diabetes is a lifelong disease. You do not "outgrow" it as I am so frequently asked by people, and you cannot rid yourself of it through diet and exercise, although both are critical in controlling your blood sugar levels.

It is a disease that does not discriminate on the basis of sex, color, or age, although it typically appears in childhood, giving it its common name of juvenile diabetes. It does not discriminate on the basis of social status, wealth, or celebrity status either. Many high-profile celebrities, such as Nick Jonas of the Jonas Brothers and heavy-metal rocker Bret Michaels, have type 1 diabetes.

Mary Tyler Moore, my personal hero in the war on type 1 diabetes, is both a diabetic herself and the International Chairperson for the Juvenile Diabetes Research Foundation. Ms. Moore's candidness in describing her own struggles with type 1 diabetes, and her willingness to work so hard for the cause, serves as an inspiration to all affected by the disease.

Although great strides have been made toward improving the life of diabetics with new types of insulin, improved blood glucose testing and monitoring devices, and greater success with transplantation, a cure still eludes us. Regardless, we have come a very long way; before the discovery of insulin in the early 1920s, starvation was often prescribed as a treatment for type 1 diabetes and a diagnosis of diabetes was a certain death sentence.

Today, type 1 diabetics are living more comfortably through the introduction of the insulin pump, which delivers insulin through an infusion site beneath the skin which eliminates the need for syringes, improved blood glucose meters that require smaller quantities of blood and deliver more accurate results, and continuous glucose monitors, important to people who have lost their ability to sense blood sugar lows or for people who might need tighter monitoring, such as infants or pregnant women.

In 1998 Dr. James Shapiro performed the first human islet transplantation using a less-toxic immune-suppressing drug that greatly improves the success rate of transplanted insulin-producing cells. In 2006 the first generation of continuous glucose monitors received approval from the U.S. Food and Drug Administration for use in type 1 diabetics. And today (2011) researchers are close to perfecting the first artificial pancreas that integrates the insulin pump with the continuous glucose monitor to replicate the body's pancreatic function.

Still, none of these is a cure, and doctors and researchers continue to test new drugs and experiment with existing drugs to search for one that can arrest or even reverse the pancreas' loss of function. The long-term health effects of juvenile diabetes are devastating and costly, both financially and emotionally. As a parent, I find it so difficult to see my child suffer.

~Lori Dotson, Edgewood, New Mexico, September 13, 2011

1 DIAGNOSIS

The girl lay near motionless on the hospital gurney, her labored breathing barely audible over the constant beep of the monitors, a skeleton of a child clinging to life, dark rings circling her eyes, cheeks sunken like Edvard Munch's *The Scream* from a century ago, a terrifying sight to any parent.

"What is it? What's wrong with my daughter?" I asked the resident physician.

"Diabetes, ma'am, your daughter has diabetes," he replied flatly.

"Okay, so what else can it be?" I said, disbelieving.

"Ma'am, this is the classic presentation of type 1 diabetes," he said, now in a tone of great sadness.

Noticeably relieved that she did not have cancer or some other *serious* disease, I quietly wondered why the doctor and two nurses standing nearby seemed so sad. I vaguely remembered a kid from my childhood who would visit the school nurse each day before lunch for an insulin injection, an inconvenience maybe but not a big deal. I found myself lost in thought for several minutes.

Less than an hour earlier, clad in my over-sized black and white vertically-striped jersey, black knee-highs, and silver whistle, I was readying myself to referee my 9-year-old son's soccer game when I could barely make out the muffled jingle of my cell phone in the distance. I jogged over to my bright yellow duffel, the one they give all coaches and referees, and clumsily fumbled through spare clothing, stakes, and flags in search of my phone. Had the call come any later, I would have missed it completely as we were only moments away from the coin toss and official start of the game, the final one of the season.

"Hello?" I said, completely unprepared for the words that would follow.

"Lori, now I don't want you to panic, but they are taking Kaitlin to the University of New Mexico Hospital by ambulance..." my husband Rick began.

"What? Why? Is she okay?" I immediately interrupted.

"Just stay calm. Drive safe. And meet me near the ambulance entrance on the south side of the hospital." He said in a steady voice, always the calm one.

I immediately disobeyed. Frantic, I uttered some unintelligible words to the coach about refereeing the game and taking my son home and then scooped up my duffel and scampered over to my vehicle, shaking and crying, not really understanding what Rick had just said. I hopped into my Honda Pilot and backed up without looking, robotically going through the driving motions, feeling like I was watching this all unfold on television, a true out-of-body experience.

As if transported by H.G. Wells' time machine, I suddenly found myself near the ambulance entrance to the hospital with no recollection of how I go there; to this day, I do not remember the seven-mile drive from the soccer fields down to UNM Hospital. I briefly caught a glimpse of my precious daughter as they wheeled the gurney inside, bags of fluid hanging high above her soft blonde head, a white sheet draped over her tiny trunk.

Entering through the side door, I nearly collided with Rick who apparently saw me coming and must have sensed my shock and confusion because he guided me over to an isolated glass room in the ER where they had just taken Kaitlin.

"She's okay, Lori. Just calm down. Everything is going to be okay." He reassured me.

For the next four hours we stood in the ER while the doctors and nurses attempted to stabilize my daughter. Only in hindsight did I realize just how serious her condition actually was. My ignorance was truly a blessing in this case.

Kaitlin was admitted to the hospital with a severe case of ketoacidosis, a condition most common in people with untreated type 1 diabetes mellitus, formerly referred to as juvenile diabetes, and also known as insulin-dependent diabetes. Common signs of diabetic ketoacidosis, or DKA, include extreme fatigue and weight loss as the insulin deficiency causes the body to metabolize or literally *eat* away at its own muscle tissue rather than consume glucose for energy, leaving a fruity smell on the breath as if the person has just drank a bottle of wine. Other symptoms include loss of appetite, abdominal pain, excessive thirst, and frequent urination. In advanced stages, the person has shortness of breath, literally gasping for air, and may even begin vomiting. Left untreated, DKA can lead to a coma and even death.

For four hours we watched the digital display on the monitors in the ER, her blood sugar hovering around 400, her heart rate and blood pressure persistently high, a body under stress. At one point, I recall asking the doctor why they had not given her any insulin because that much I knew about diabetes—that she needed insulin. He replied that they needed to stabilize and rehydrate her before they could begin to treat the diabetes.

After the initial shock and confusion had subsided, a nurse came over to talk to us. As if reading from a script, she asked us several questions related to family history—did we have any other family members with diabetes? Did autoimmune disorders run in our family? Did we notice that she was drinking more often or visiting the restroom more frequently?

I think it was at this point, or sometime soon afterward, that I began to feel an extreme sense of guilt over missing the warning signs of my daughter's disease. How did I not notice her weight loss, which had become quite substantial, or the fact that she was drinking constantly? How did I allow this to become a life-threatening situation? What an awful mother I must be. Was I paying more attention to my job than my children? The guilt would stay with me for a very long time.

With no family history, it is easy to miss the warning signs of juvenile diabetes; the signs of Kaitlin's diabetes were missed even by the professionals. I had taken Kaitlin to the doctor several times in the previous year for seemingly unrelated symptoms, which with benefit of hindsight, I now realize were related to her diabetes. Never once did a doctor think to test her blood sugar, which is astonishing given the relative simplicity of the test, a simple prick of the finger to obtain a mere smidgen of blood to test with a hand-held meter.

Less than a year earlier, Kaitlin had contracted a skin virus on her foot that refused to go away and given what I know now, this virus was likely the environmental *trigger* for the onset of her disease. She also had an overwhelming fatigue and moodiness that I thought might be signs of depression which runs in my family. I was concerned enough to ask our pediatrician about it, but he seemed hesitant to prescribe anything for a child so young. Fortunately (or maybe not) these were all signs of high blood sugar related to diabetes and not of a deep dark depression that had tortured so many of my relatives, claiming the lives of two of my cousins years earlier.

Many, many signs were missed, which I think was due, in part, to denial. Several weeks before her diagnosis, I had mentioned to Rick that our daughter was drinking constantly, which is a tell-tale sign of diabetes, and in a tone that bordered on anger, which was very unusual for my normally laid-back husband, he stated emphatically, "that girl is not a diabetic!"

In the weeks that followed, I became accustomed to the frequent drinking and because she was a pre-teen, I didn't think twice about the time she spent in the bathroom. She had begun menstruating just a few months earlier so I assumed the frequent trips to the bathroom were all part of *tween* self-discovery and I respected her privacy.

The skin virus mentioned earlier actually began about ten months before her diagnosis, following a ski trip up at Sandia Peak, about twenty minutes from our house. At first, I thought it was just some type of rash or skin irritation related to too-tight ski boots, but as time went on, and as doctors began to prescribe increasingly more powerful steroidal creams, I realized it was much more than that.

Researchers have theorized that diabetes may lie dormant in the body until triggered by an environmental stimulus, and it's quite possible that this skin virus was the *trigger* for the onset of her illness. Many parents have reported that their child had some type of lingering virus right before their diagnosis. Looking back on the months that followed, it is apparent that Kaitlin was beginning to experience more and more symptoms after that rash first appeared, the symptoms increasing almost asymptotically, until that fateful day in October when she lie gasping for air in the ER.

Recently, I learned that cold weather might be another trigger, which I found interesting because the onset of Kaitlin's diabetes was quite possibly that previous winter following our ski outing. Furthermore, researchers have discovered that type 1 diabetes develops more frequently during the winter months and is more common in colder climates.

Researchers also believe that some people are genetically predisposed to becoming type 1 diabetics, that they will get the disease at some point in their life, usually but not always during childhood, and hence, the name *juvenile* diabetes. They can do nothing to prevent it.

Becoming educated about my child's disease helped me to overcome much of the guilt I felt in the year following her diagnosis. It seems ridiculous to me now, but early on, I believed I had done something to make her diabetic, like feeding her too much pasta or letting her skip the vegetables on occasion. I now know that Kaitlin would have developed this disease eventually and I was helpless to prevent it. Researchers have discovered that most people who get type 1 actually have certain auto-antibodies in their blood for years before the onset of the disease.

With as much as the medical community knows about juvenile diabetes, there is still much more they do not understand. My daughter seemed to have none of the risk factors, other than being a member of the Caucasian race, which has a disproportionate number of cases. There is a very strong genetic component to the disease, but we have absolutely no family history. And scientists believe that early diet may play a role as it appears to be less common in those who were breastfed and consumed their first solid foods at an older age. However, Kaitlin was breastfed the first six or seven months of her life and was barely eating solid foods by her first birthday while my son, who has not developed the disease, was only breastfed the first 10 weeks of his life and began eating solids at four months of age.

There are still so many unanswered questions about the disease and so many opposing theories. The best that a family can do is to become educated on blood sugar management and pray for a cure.

2 ONE DAY EARLIER

"What do you mean she's still in bed? Put her on the phone" I said with irritation.

My son Corey was already awake when I left the hotel room an hour earlier, but Kaitlin was the picture of pure exhaustion, not that it surprised me much. She had been sleeping in for months. It was a real chore to get her up in the morning for school, truly living up to her stereotype of the pubescent girl refusing to get out of bed in the morning.

"What mama? I'm tired." Said the slow-motion voice on the other end of the phone.

"Honey, we're going to have a lot of fun today in Vegas after I finish up this meeting so get up, take a shower, and get dressed. Okay?" I said with authority.

"We're going to the top of the Stratosphere Tower and to see the animal acts at Circus Circus. There's Siegfried & Roy's Secret Garden and Dolphin Habitat and the M&M Store, four floors of M&Ms! Doesn't that sound exciting?" I think I heard her mutter an okay, but I couldn't be sure. Her voice was so small.

After my meeting, I called the hotel room again to let the kids know I would be back as soon as I talked to a few more people. "What? She's still asleep" I said to my son in astonishment. At this point, I decided to skip the after-meeting meetings and head straight back to the hotel, letting my colleagues know that I needed to leave because my daughter might be sick back at the hotel.

When I returned to the room, Corey looked a little bored, fiddling with his electronic gadgets while Kaitlin continued to sleep, literally in the same position as when I left.

"Come on, Kaitlin. What's the problem? I said.

"I'm tired, mama." She said with true fatigue in her voice.

I checked her forehead—no fever, no outward signs of illness, just fatigue. We needed to check out of the hotel soon and we would be leaving that evening anyway so I hurried the kids out of the room for the start of our day's adventure.

Soon we were up and out of the room without a complaint, but with each stop we made, Kaitlin would find a comfortable place to sit and fall into a comfortable slumber. As Corey and I circled the Stratosphere, taking in the 360-degree views of Las Vegas, Kaitlin found a bench and went to sleep. I was convinced she was getting sick, possibly the flu, I thought. Maybe the other flu symptoms would appear that evening or the next day. It was puzzling that she didn't have any other symptoms.

Next we went to a large indoor amusement park on the Strip that even had an indoor roller coaster. I thought that Kaitlin, always the thrill seeker, would jump at the chance to test her nerves on the coaster with its steep descents and loop-di-loops, certainly not for me, but she loved this stuff. Instead, she sat down at a bench and laid her head on the adjoining table and for the next hour she slept while Corey enjoyed ride after ride. He would frequently rush back to tell Kaitlin how much fun it was, eagerly trying to coax her into joining him, but he was barely able to garner a response.

Even though our plane was not departing for another 6 hours, it was clear that we needed to get to the airport and get home. Disappointed but very understanding, we left what Corey called "the greatest indoor amusement park he had ever seen" and headed for the airport. The short trip to the airport was very quiet. I was puzzled by this illness Kaitlin had—no fever, no symptoms other than fatigue, but clearly something was wrong.

Finally understanding the severity of her condition, I stopped at a gas station on the way to the airport and considered searching for a clinic. I was getting scared now. It's hard to know how to react to something you've never seen before. Kaitlin was clearly behaving out of character. She was never one to keep her illnesses quiet—if she was sick, everyone knew it! But on this day, she was very quiet and lethargic with no plausible explanation available.

Las Vegas is a big, exciting place with neon everywhere, busy streets, and even busier sidewalks. I just wanted to leave. Even Corey wanted to leave. We understood now that something was wrong with Kaitlin and we needed to be home.

At the airport, I tried unsuccessfully to book us on an earlier flight. Hour upon hour passed as we sat in the hard black chairs that lined the airport terminal, delicately holding my baby girl who so obviously had something wrong with her. Corey and I were uncharacteristically quiet and stayed that way for a very long time.

Exhausted from our trip, we arrived back home around eleven in the evening. My husband was eagerly awaiting our arrival. I had already told him that Kaitlin had fallen ill. However, when we arrived he looked horrified. We put the kids to bed and discussed Kaitlin's condition.

"She looks like a skeleton, Lori." Rick said in horror.

I could say nothing.

It was true. In just a couple of days, she had lost considerably more weight and now looked like skin and bones. The initial transformation was so slow that neither of us noticed the weight loss, but now her condition was accelerating. We made up our minds that Rick would take her to the doctor the next morning, Saturday, and I would continue our normal routine and take my son to his soccer game.

3 HOSPITAL STAY

After some period of time in the ER, insulin was gradually introduced through Kaitlin's IV line and we began to see some relief in her blood sugar levels. Soon afterward a nurse informed us they would be moving Kaitlin to the pediatric ICU and that we should anticipate a one-week hospital stay. Although "ICU" had a serious ring to it, I was somewhat relieved that the doctors felt she was stable enough to move to another part of the hospital. Plus, I just didn't like the ER for some reason.

The pediatric ICU was on the fourth floor of the hospital and from the large picture window on the wall opposite the door, there was a marvelous view. I was allowed to stay with my daughter day and night, sleeping on a tiny mattress next to that large picture window, not nearly enough room for a big person, but my 5-foot-3 frame fit nicely in the space. I slept with one eye closed, one eye on my daughter as she lay there asleep for most of the next three days.

As monitors continued to flash her vital signs, the room was never completely dark, and an occasional beep or alarm would alert the nurse and cause my heart to skip a beat or two. But looking back on it all now, I actually have quite fond memories of the ICU. The nurses who attended to my daughter were topnotch, true professionals, and I loved every single one of them. Each one cared for my daughter as if she were their own.

Most of the next three days in the ICU were a blur with a few notable exceptions which I remember quite vividly. The first was when I saw our future president's motorcade traveling down Lomas Boulevard on its way to the UNM football stadium for a pre-election rally. It was night-time, things were quiet in the ICU, and the lights were mostly off. My mind started drifting from my body as I stared blankly out the large picture window beside my makeshift bed when I noticed a tight and orderly procession of nearly identical, dark-colored vehicles slowly passing on the street below. I knew that someone very important must be visiting UNM. In the distance, I could see the lights of the football stadium and although I could not hear the crowd, in my mind, I could hear the cheers and feel the excitement. Only later did I learn that Barack Obama had a rally at UNM that evening.

My second vivid memory was of an experience that occurred very late one night, possibly the wee hours of the morning, although I literally had no sense of time during my stay in the ICU. I was in a quasi-sleep state when I began to feel the room vibrate gently and in an instant, I knew that a helicopter had landed on the roof. We must have been situated directly below the bulls-eye because it felt like it landed right on the floor above us. Later I found out that a trauma case was flown in that evening. UNM Hospital is the only hospital in Albuquerque, only hospital in the entire State of New Mexico, to have a trauma center, and so all cases end up there.

Time had no meaning when we were at the hospital, night, day, early, late, one day, two days. It was mostly a blur. I don't even remember eating, but I'm sure that I did. My husband stayed one night when I had to go home to finish a report for work. I don't remember writing the report, but I know that I did. I don't even remember what day I left to do that or how long I was gone.

After the third day in the ICU, Kaitlin was transferred to a regular hospital room and we were told we'd be in the hospital another week, which seemed a little excessive to me. Things weren't too bad for awhile as a seemingly constant stream of visitors would cycle through—school friends, cousins, teachers, grandma, granny, papa, her aunts and uncles. Kaitlin was smiling again and she was finally awake and even talking! Gifts and flowers arrived nonstop and she was eating real food and for a short while it seemed like life was getting back to normal.

We walked down to the children's playroom, Kaitlin in her fuzzy slippers, pushing the metal device which held her bag of IV fluids, and she really seemed okay. We saw many other children who were not okay, children bald from chemotherapy, children relegated to wheelchairs, children obviously the victims of domestic violence, and my eyes welled up with tears. I felt so lucky, so blessed, that my daughter was okay.

Halloween was right around the corner and the nurse was passing out new pillow cases for all the kids, black pillow cases with bright orange candy corns on them. There were sugary cookies and baskets of candy for everyone and this was when we realized how different things would be in the future. How cruel to be diagnosed with diabetes the week before Halloween! Regardless, the whole family was very happy to see Kaitlin smiling and moving about after several days glued to her bed.

Then, just as we thought life might become somewhat normal again, we were visited by the diabetes educator, and this is where the work was to begin. The whole family, my 9–year-old son included, would need to become "re-educated" on our new life, our new life with diabetes. Alas, I finally understood why they told us we would be in the hospital for another week because it would take that long to learn this whole new regimen of insulin injections, blood sugar testing, and carbohydrate counting. It was initially overwhelming.

I never have liked needles much and I think the same is true of my husband, but the first thing the diabetes educator (nurse) taught us was how to give each other shots in the belly using saline solution. As Kaitlin enjoyed her new found celebrity status back in her private hospital room, my husband and I were tucked away in another room, poking each other with syringes, all the while being critiqued by our diabetes educator. I recall there were three other people at that initial educational session, all watching us closely, each one trying to figure out just how quickly we might catch on to all of this, but all incredibly supportive, as well. I remember being so nervous that I would make a mistake, that the nurses would think I was stupid, and I felt a lot of pressure to do things right.

Each day we would have another training session of increasing difficulty. On the second day, Kaitlin joined in. On the third day, our son Corey joined in. It was very important that the entire family understood how this all worked. The nurses all seemed genuinely pleased with our progress, but then we had one last hurdle to clear. Kaitlin had to give *herself* a real injection. It was okay to inject an orange or inject a parent with saline, but to inject herself with real insulin seemed to create a bit of a problem for her. If we could just accomplish this one seemingly simple task, we could finally go home. At every meal, the nurse would ask if Kaitlin was doing her own injections yet, and we would regretfully say no.

Although it seemed like a long time, we were only in the hospital for a total of one week, including the ER, ICU, and the children's ward. We were finally released late one evening after it was concluded that Kaitlin sort of gave herself an injection.

4 WELCOME HOME

"Mom, can I have *anything* on the menu?" said the wonderfully precocious little boy with a mop of thick brown hair a top is head.

"Sure Corey. In honor of Kaitlin's return from the hospital, you can have *anything* on the menu. I don't care what it costs." I said, seemingly without a care in the world.

"Um, Mom…"

"What Kaitlin?"

"I forgot my insulin," she said in a voice flush with guilt and disappointment.

Barely a week had passed while we were in the hospital, a week with no real contact with the outside world other than our hospital visitors, a surreal journey that left the whole family mentally drained. Little did we know that the "surreal journey" had just begun and that life as we had known it before was gone forever.

Just leaving the house was now a challenge—we had to take a stock of supplies with us everywhere we went—syringes, alcohol wipes, vials of Novolog insulin, a glucagon kit, sugary snacks, blood glucose meter, test strips, extra batteries, sharps container, ice packs to keep the Novolog cool.

My gosh! Did people actually do this? This was a whole new world that I had never even imagined! But that was just the beginning. As we would soon learn, managing those blood sugars was the real challenge. One minute Kaitlin was at 378 and then next she was 52.

Unfortunately, we have been living with this disease for nearly three years now and I cannot say that her blood sugars are ever really under control, at least not what I would consider control, although Kaitlin does experience stretches of time where her sugars are relatively stable. Then she will get sick or be premenstrual or be otherwise stressed, and her blood sugars will shoot through the roof. On the opposite end of the spectrum, she has experienced significant lows when she was actively dancing or participating on the cross-country team. Although managing blood sugars is difficult for any diabetic, I think it is particularly difficult for children because of their sporadic schedules, changing bodies, and raging hormones.

Without her vial of Novolog, I felt naked, vulnerable, and I could see that Kaitlin felt the same. We packed up our belongings, left the restaurant, and drove the 25-plus miles back to our home in Edgewood. It really put a damper on the day. Corey was very understanding but he clearly understood that things would be much different from now on.

For one of the first times in my life, I was unsure what to do. I'm not talking about this one *particular* moment at the restaurant. I'm talking about *in general.* Still feeling very guilty over missing the signs and symptoms of my daughter's diabetes, I worried about everything now. Thus, it was very important to me that we immediately go back home where we had vials of Novolog stacked neatly in the refrigerator. I remember feeling that it was a mistake to leave the house and that we should be home where it was *safe.*

We did eventually go out to a restaurant again. We even took family trips. But just when I would start feeling comfortable that things were under control, another crisis would ultimately arise.

5 NIGHT-TIME SCARY-TIME

Lying next to my naked breast, sheets wet with spilled milk, a white crust formed neatly around her lips, Kaitlin lay next to me in bed, both of us exhausted to the world. She was barely two months old, a very clingy baby who enjoyed the comfort of her mother. Countless times I would awaken during the night, startled by the limp and lifeless mass next to me, afraid I may have rolled over on her, snuffing out her tiny existence, and immediately I would rock her into wakefulness. Each time she would stretch and open her little eyes with that same groggy, totally relaxed demeanor of a baby drunk on her mamma's milk. She loved to sleep, sleep next to mamma, but mamma didn't sleep much.

Twelve years later, mamma still wasn't sleeping much. For the mother of a child with diabetes, night-time is the scariest time of day, especially within the first couple months of diagnosis. In bits and spurts, the diabetic child's pancreas tries to eke out a little more insulin, maybe 30% of its function still remaining. Once the body becomes bathed in the artificially-introduced insulin, the relieved pancreas gets a second wind and its insulin production is unpredictable. Unfortunately, the body cannot effectively rid itself of this excess insulin and the child's blood sugars can quickly drop. While high blood sugars are damaging to your body over time, low blood sugars are much more dangerous, potentially leading to unconsciousness and even death.

For the first three months of Kaitlin's life, I would lie awake staring at her, checking her breathing, watching her chest move up and down. For the first three months of Kaitlin's life with diabetes, I would lie awake staring at her, checking her breathing, watching her chest move up and down. The baby Kaitlin slept next to me in my bed; the adolescent Kaitlin slept next to me in her own bed. Soon the time of day meant nothing to me, sleeping whenever was convenient, whenever I was sure my baby was okay. She will always be my baby.

When a child is first diagnosed with type 1, the doctors and nurses are very conservative with the amount of insulin they prescribe and for good reason. The doctors and nurses are trying desperately to avoid "insulin shock" where the child is given too much insulin and their blood sugar drops to a level that might cause unconsciousness or even death. If a child is unconscious, they cannot ingest the *antidote*—that is, the sugary drink or tablet that will raise their blood sugar. In such an instance, the only option is to give them a glucagon injection, and we have several glucagon injection kits, one at home, one at school, and one at Granny's house. However, if the child is still conscious but not quite capable of drinking a sugary drink or eating a piece of candy, you can squeeze cake icing between their cheek and gums and let it dissolve and slide down their throat. Luckily, we have never had to experience either of these last two situations.

As much as I hate high blood sugar, because I know the havoc it wreaks on the body, I hate low blood sugar much more. Low blood sugar can kill you immediately while it takes years of high blood sugars to do their damage. So what is low blood sugar, or hypoglycemia? Well, it's commonly defined as a blood glucose (sugar) level below 70 milligrams per deciliter (mg/dl), and its symptoms vary among people. The diabetic child and their parents soon learn to recognize the unique signs associated with their low blood sugars. For example, Kaitlin's mild low blood sugars typically reveal themselves through hunger, while more severe sugar lows turn her into a drunken sailor, laughing wildly, stumbling across the room, and slurring her speech.

Symptoms of mild low blood sugar include nausea, extreme hunger, nervousness, clammy skin or excessive sweating, rapid heartbeat (tachycardia), numbness or tingling of the fingertips or lips, and trembling. Moderate hypoglycemia, defined as blood sugars below 55 mg/dl, will begin to affect the central nervous system, causing mood changes, such as irritability, anxiety, restlessness, or anger, and also confusion, inability to concentrate, blurred vision, dizziness, headache, loss of motor coordination, and extreme fatigue.

Kaitlin is typically unaware of her low blood sugar until it is below about 60 mg/dl at which point she will become very hungry. She has experienced several blood sugar lows in the middle of the night—often she will wake up hungry and not quite feeling right and her sugar will be in the low 50s. However, I have waken her in the middle of the night for a routine reading and discovered her sugar in the 50s, which is very alarming, especially since there are usually several hours left before morning, meaning that she had the potential to drop much lower. To combat these middle-of-the-night lows, we are now able to adjust her basal insulin at night-time because she is on an insulin pump. But for the first 8 months following her diagnosis we did not have this luxury because she was still doing injections.

On the severe end of the spectrum, a blood sugar below 40 mg/dl can cause seizures, convulsions, and loss of consciousness (coma). Physiologically, the body's temperature drops (hypothermia) and prolonged severe hypoglycemia can cause irreversible brain damage and heart problems. If emergency medical treatment is not provided, severe hypoglycemia can be fatal. Kaitlin has experienced a handful of blood sugar measurements in this range, one was 37 mg/dl, which merely made her act like a very happy drunk and another was 32 mg/dl and she felt faint, was noticeably trembling and unable to pour her own drink.

I must caution that each person is different and just because Kaitlin was still functioning with a blood sugar in the 30s does not mean that others would be quite so lucky. I have heard anecdotes of people being unconscious with a blood sugar in the 40s. On the other hand, I've heard people say that they measured their sugars into the low 20s and were still functional so there are definitely no hard and fast rules here. All blood sugars below 70 mg/dl need to be treated seriously.

The standard method of treating a blood sugar low is to ingest 15 grams (g) of a fast-acting carbohydrate, such as 4 ounces of apple juice, a piece of candy, or a glucose tablet, and then waiting 15 minutes before retesting. If the blood sugar is still under 70 after 15 minutes, 15 additional grams of carbohydrate should be ingested. However, our experience has been that 15 g is usually more than enough to raise the blood sugar to a safe range. It is important not to over-treat the low blood sugar, which creates a viscous cycle of highs and lows.

It's also important to know the factors that contribute to low blood sugar so that you can check more frequently during these situations. Some of these factors are well known, such as skipping meals, getting extra exercise, taking insulin and then forgetting to eat, or accidentally injecting too much insulin. However, some of the lesser known causes of low blood sugar include severe infection, drinking alcohol, and taking certain drugs, such as beta blockers and certain antibiotics, which is why a diabetic needs to be extra concerned about the side effects of all drugs that he or she is taking. Yes, your doctor and pharmacist have a responsibility, but ultimately, you need to be an informed patient, or an informed parent of a diabetic child.

A really sad story told to me soon after Kaitlin was diagnosed with diabetes was that of a loving mother of two young boys who suffered from type 1 diabetes for most of her life. One evening she decided to have some wine before bedtime, and apparently, her blood sugar had dropped to a critically low level during the night because she could not be awakened the next morning. The saddest part about it was that it was her two young sons who discovered that she was dead. Their dad had already left for work and the boys alerted the neighbors when they couldn't wake their mother. Alcohol and insulin-dependent (type 1) diabetes do not mix. Not only does alcohol lower your blood sugar, but it also interferes with your ability to sense your blood sugar lows, and this is a fatal combination.

Fortunately, today there are continuous glucose monitors that can be programmed to alert the patient of when their blood sugar is outside of a specified range of say 70-150 mg/dl. But unfortunately, unlike an insulin pump, continuous glucose monitors are not typically covered by most insurance and are quite costly. However, for people with low blood sugar unawareness, the device keeps them alive. Fortunately, technology is developing so rapidly that in a matter of a few years, the insulin pump and continuous glucose monitor should be sufficiently integrated to take some of the guess-work out of this. The so-called artificial pancreas could revolutionize the life of the type 1 diabetic.

6 SHATTERED

"Ever since Kaitlin got her diabetes, you ignore me. I don't get to do anything anymore all because of her diabetes…" said the little boy in frustration.

Corey finally spoke up and he left me a little stunned. It was true. We didn't do the things we used to do anymore because it was too difficult or impossible.

So now, not only did I feel guilt over my daughter's diabetes, I also felt guilt over not paying enough attention to my son. I felt guilt over working full-time. I felt guilt over sometimes coming up short at all of these things. And although the community of parents of diabetic children was very supportive, I felt very alone because I did not seek help. The resources were all there, but instead I just let this all build inside of me. Maybe I thought I could handle it.

I continued to work full-time at my job as a scientist for a large federal contractor, which wasn't too difficult at first because I telecommuted. My work arrangement allowed me to run over to Kaitlin's elementary school during the day to give her an injection of insulin when it was required, or to be alerted when the opposite problem occurred, a blood sugar low caused from too much insulin.

I frequently ended up taking Kaitlin home from school and she missed much of the second half of her sixth-grade year. Fortunately, my daughter's elementary school has wonderful teachers and staff and they helped us through these difficult times. Many at the school had experienced this in the past with other students and even their own family members and their love and support will always be cherished and remembered.

Unfortunately, life at work wasn't as easy. I'm not sure that anyone other than my immediate supervisor even knew what happened to my daughter or understood the effect it had on my life. In hindsight, maybe I should have requested family leave to care for my daughter (and myself). Physically and emotionally I was breaking down. But that is not what I did and it changed my future.

About 3 months following Kaitlin's diagnosis, after months of lying awake, watching over her, quietly deliberating whether or not to wake her to check her blood sugar, I had grown tired and my patience had grown thin. I had an unfortunate incident take place with a male colleague that I am not at liberty to discuss openly, not that I would really want to relive that nightmare anyway.

This one incident destroyed my credibility and my career and left me with a feeling despair. My work life crumbled around me and feeling I could do nothing right, this became a self-fulfilling prophecy, to a certain extent. Once honored by our company's vice president, once the recipient of plaques and awards by managers and congressmen, I had become the pariah of my organization. This was especially damaging to my psyche since I've always placed a high emphasis on having positive interpersonal relationships with everyone in my life, at work or at home.

With my self-esteem and self-worth rapidly declining, a *melancholy* began to seep into my life. I desperately fought it through intense physical exercise, running the rough and rugged trails by my house for miles and miles through mud and snow, riding my mountain and road bikes to exhaustion, refusing to even take a break when I traveled for my job when I would run on the hotel's treadmill until I crashed on the hotel bed, which also helped me to deal with the fact that I was away from my family.

One day, following an especially long hard bike ride, I moved the wrong way in the shower, and an intense pain, the likes of which I had never felt before, rippled throughout my entire lower back. I fell to the shower floor and could not get up. This was the start of a back problem that would persist for a very long time. This was also the start of a downward depressive spiral from which I would not truly escape until several months after I left my job.

7 VACATION

The road trip through Washington State was simply majestic. Jagged mountains of the Cascade Range piercing fluffy clouds which captured our imaginations as we traveled south from Seattle, snippets of white capped waves were visible between trees of the forest as we traveled north up the coastline, and everywhere we discovered quaint little villages with their share of eccentric locals. Even the larger cities were beautiful in their own special way.

Kaitlin had started on her insulin pump just a month earlier and the new found freedom was exhilarating, no more syringes, vials of Novolog, or ice packs to keep it chilled. She looked like any other 12-year-old, except she wore a device on her belt that looked like an iPod, actually making her look quite hip. We were able to participate in all the normal activities that a family on vacation would engage in. Kaitlin simply disconnected her pump to go swimming in the pool or ocean, and every 2 to 3 days she changed her *infusion* site where the insulin enters her body.

We hit all of the major attractions in the greater Seattle area, climbing the 2-story high rock wall at the REI store, riding the simulator at the aircraft museum, racing little stock cars at the indoor NASCAR track in Bellevue where they actually let the kids reach speeds of up to 50 mph. Even after my son Corey crashed into a barrier going about 40 mph, they continued to let him drive, not that he really wanted to after that!

I had been to Seattle a couple times previously, but I never realized all the things there were to see and do. The Pike Place market was much more exciting than I had remembered. You could not walk down the road without bumping into a street performer or two, whereas my recollection from 20 years ago was mostly of a row of dead fish hanging up inside several large canvas tents. Then again, everything I do seems ten times better when I am with my kids.

I am blessed with two great children who appreciate fine music and Seattle has a little something for everyone. My husband and son are the musicians in the family, hammering away on their guitars and drums, playing music a little too heavy for me, but I love it nonetheless. Anyway, Seattle is simply a Mecca for anyone who enjoys new music and not surprisingly, it is everywhere, just like the coffee, another one of my favorites.

The kids were quite happy to see water, too. We live in a desert (New Mexico) so you can imagine how exciting water might be, not just the Pacific Ocean, but also the tour boats on Lake Washington between Seattle and Bellevue and the ferries that carry you and your car between Bainbridge Island and Seattle and *wow*, what cheap entertainment!

I was so excited to take my kids to Mount Rainier. Twenty years earlier on a business trip to Seattle, I climbed Mount Rainier with a couple friends of mine who lived in the area. Being a geologist, I am simply in love with mountains. I cannot get enough of them. And being a lifelong athlete, I enjoy new athletic challenges so climbing Mount Rainier was a very natural thing to do. Unfortunately, this didn't work out quite so well when I tried to do it with the kids. Little did I realize just how strenuous uphill hiking could be and we were continuously *feeding* Kaitlin's blood sugar lows.

Prior to our climb, we had lunch in the appropriately-named *Paradise Inn* and Kaitlin *bolused* (i.e., gave herself insulin) in an amount necessary to cover the carbohydrates she consumed. Still being somewhat new to this, she religiously counted her carbs and bolused the appropriate amount giving little consideration to the amount of physical activity she was getting. Starting our climb with her blood sugar hovering around 120 proved disastrous as we found ourselves continually *feeding* her to keep her in the normal range. Finally, she hit a low in the 50s and we decided that maybe climbing Mount

Rainier wasn't such a grand idea after all. Well, at least we have an excuse to return some day!

The next major stop was Ocean Shores, a town that's difficult to describe, like a resort *ghost* town, several luxurious (and empty) hotels lined the beach, the landscape dotted with *For Sale* signs. Although we were in a real estate bust at the time, I had the distinct impression that this place had gone bust years earlier. But the lack of people was a blessing. We had our own private little beach where we built castles, buried each other in the sand, and ran in and out of the frigid waves.

We rented bikes and rode all over town with little worry about traffic but a lot of worry about low blood sugars as we made many frequent stops at the store to pick up sweets for Kaitlin. This was certainly the longest period of time we had been away from home since her diagnosis about 8 months previous, and all and all, we were handling things very well. And it felt good to get away from my job, if only for a week.

The first family vacation in quite some time was actually going very well. And we were just getting to the good part—vampires! Kaitlin, the self-proclaimed vampire lover (or is it werewolf lover?) was so excited when we arrived in Forks, the hometown of Bella of *Twilight* fame. Even Corey was excited to see the places talked about in the Stephanie Meyer books and movies. I really could not have asked for a better vacation. Being there with my kids and sharing in their excitement, I found it almost possible to ignore the constant spasms in my lower back.

Final stop on the *Twilight* tour was Port Angeles. Little did I know that in addition to being a hotspot for *Twilight* enthusiasts, Port Angeles is also the departure point for people cruising up to Alaska, and as such, the hotel rooms were scarce when we arrived and prices were outrageously expensive. I had to pull out all of the punches, but somehow I negotiated a $200/night room down to $120.

Anyway, Port Angeles was a great little port town, and after we finished our business there, we drove up to Hurricane Ridge, part of Washington's Olympic National Park. The drive to the top took considerably longer than one would expect as the road winded through thick forests, enveloped by long tree limbs that threatened to toss out a squirrel or two without warning. While the kids played on their various electronic gadgets (thankfully with the volume turned off), I relaxed and fantasized about a life far away from people, away from the emotional pain of my job, living in harmony with nature, and before long, we had reached the top.

What a spectacular view. And what a lot of wind! I thought Edgewood, New Mexico, was bad, but it's nothing compared to Hurricane Ridge! We hiked again as the kids whined about having to hike everywhere, but in the end they enjoyed it just as much as I did. And this time, our hike involved no elevation change, just a simple cruise along the rocky ridge and Kaitlin's blood sugars were just fine. Everything was okay again.

We spent several hours hiking, listening to ranger-led educational programs so that the kids could earn their junior ranger badges, eating and relaxing at the Hurricane Ridge visitor's center, and buying a few obligatory T-shirts at the gift shop. We had a very enjoyable day, but the drive ahead was over 3 hours so we needed to get a move on as the sun was already melting on the horizon.

Descending the windy road from Hurricane Ridge, the kids read and quietly engaged their electronic devices as I again drifted into a fantasy world, living in a remote mountain retreat with not a care in the world, and even with a bad back the 3-hour drive to our hotel near the Bainbridge ferry seemed to pass quickly. A couple times I asked the kids if they were hungry, but they just wanted to get to the hotel as quickly as possible.

When we arrived, I poured myself out of the bucket seat of our rented economy car and the pain in my lower back reared its ugly self, making me look more like a woman of 85 than 45. Luckily, the kids were big enough to help carry our belongings up to the room. By then everyone was quite hungry and that is when we discovered that Kaitlin had left her blood glucose meter at... you guessed it... the Hurricane Ridge visitor's center! Oh – my – gosh. I had just driven over 3 hours, pain riveting through my lower back, and my daughter had left the only device we had that could measure her blood sugar and communicate with her insulin pump. What to do, what to do, think Lori, how about cry? I stayed calm, but clearly Kaitlin was upset about this. She was sure she had left the fanny pack containing her meter and diabetic supplies slung over the chair where we had lunch, but would it really still be there? Someone could easily mistake it for a purse and steal it. And the park was closing soon so we couldn't physically make it there in time to check.

I immediately called the visitor's center at the top. I called the visitor's center at the bottom. I called every number listed in the phone book and all I ever got was an automated system. Finally, I called the emergency number because actually, this was an emergency. My daughter's medical supplies were in that bag. And finally—finally, I was able to get someone on the phone. Incredible as this may sound, the fanny pack was still slung over the chair where we left it hours earlier! Park security retrieved it for us and held it at their substation in Port Angeles. We left immediately and the return trip was just over 2 hours since we didn't need to drive all the way to the top of Hurricane Ridge. But still…

Over five hours of driving on top of several hours of hiking in the hot sun and we were finally rewarded with a well-deserved dinner in Port Angeles. I actually find it quite remarkable that the kids held off without food for that long, but I think they may have been snacking on granola bars in the back seat. Weak and fatigued, I was having some difficulty getting around because of the muscle spasms in my back, but it was refreshing to finally get out of the car and have an ice-cold tea.

After dinner in Port Angeles, I drove another 2 hours back to our hotel because we had already checked in and had left our belongings there. In hindsight, I wished we had taken everything with us, but it's difficult to think when you're in crisis mode. Anyway, the kids slept the entire ride back and we were able to catch a ferry the next morning to Seattle, keeping us on a quasi-schedule.

The ferry was one of the coolest parts of our trip. It's hard to believe people do that every day and probably never give it a second thought. The water was fresh, crisp, and inviting. We loved it. And the remainder of our vacation was about as normal as one can get. We revisited the giant REI Store where Kaitlin purchased many fine clothes and Corey marveled at all of the sporting goods spread across three floors that seemed more like a museum than a store. We continued to enjoy Seattle's best in music and other entertainment and I was in heaven with my daily java fix.

I was able to let go of work for a short time, but I knew I would soon need to return to reality, the thought of which filled me with dread.

8 GETTING PHYSICAL

Her movements on stage gave the illusion of a body devoid of bones, fluid movements that hypnotized the mind and relaxed the soul. Everyone loved to watch Kaitlin dance. She was a natural.

Kaitlin had sort of a love-hate relationship with dance. She was a ballerina at 5, quit by age 8, and took it up again at 10, but she never skipped a beat. The insulin from her diabetes caused her to put on a few extra pounds, most of which she needed anyway, but it had no effect on her dance. She was as elegant as ever.

A couple of the other dancers also had juvenile diabetes so everyone was aware of the warning signs of low blood sugar. However, when she danced her blood sugar actually went *up*, especially during performances, as her body became awash in cortisol and adrenaline, hormones responsible for the *fight or flight* response, which are released by the body under conditions of stress.

What a mess this turned out to be! High, low, high, low. Because dance classes and performances were typically held in the evening, we had to deal with blood sugars that came crashing back to earth in the middle of the night. This delayed effect caused many a sleepless night for me.

Kaitlin continued to dance for about a year following her diagnosis, a time period unfortunately characterized by her most erratic blood sugars and greatest difficulty in glucose control and management. However, her next athletic endeavor proved to be even more difficult to manage—cross-country running!

In the fall of her 7th grade year, Kaitlin made me so proud by joining the cross-country team. She joined not because she loved to run, but because she wanted to be as healthy as possible, which required *some* type of physical activity. Kaitlin by her very nature would rather isolate herself in her bedroom full of books, quietly pecking out the words of her next novel than bothering with the commotion of an athletic event. Her idea of physical activity was stroking a keyboard, not sprinting past a finish line, so when she joined the team and stuck it out for the entire season, I was very proud her.

But even a 2-mile cross-country event would quickly metabolize the sugars in her blood. Anticipation of the event would frequently drop her to below a safe blood sugar range and I recall one instance in particular where her sugar was 54 within 15 minutes of the start of the girl's race. I'm not sure anyone at these meets really understood Kaitlin's disease, but that's okay because I was always there to tell her when to check her blood sugar, when to eat a snack, and when to just take it easy.

Kaitlin struggled through several last-place finishes in cross-country. Often times I swore she let others pass her so they wouldn't feel badly about their finishing times. I quietly waited at every finish line, hoping my daughter wasn't passed out and in insulin shock somewhere along the course. But she always finished, with a smile on her face, even on the hottest days at the driest meets where the desert sands covered her sweaty body in a film of filth.

Needless to say, Kaitlin did not participate in cross-country the following year; however, she did join the tennis club and we discovered she had a natural knack for hitting little yellow balls at the other players. She went up against several boys her age and by the second half of the season, she was winning more matches than she was losing. She was the star of their final season-ending tournament and I think she felt good about that.

Blood sugar management was easier once Kaitlin was on the insulin pump because she could adjust her *basal* insulin, or amount injected to cover her normal metabolism, based on her activity levels. By this time, she was becoming quite proficient at counting carbs, estimating insulin requirements, and regularly checking her blood sugar levels. She would disconnect her pump for most rigorous physical activities to avoid damaging the device so she wouldn't even be receiving insulin at these times. This was particularly true for organized sporting events, but not always for recreational activities and one event in particular stands out as being a particularly harrowing.

We were on vacation in western New York, attending a graduation party for my cousin's daughter way out in the countryside, a couple hours from our hotel room back in Lewiston. Kaitlin and her brother Corey were enjoying a volleyball match with their second and third cousins on my dad's side of the family, the competitive side of the family. So, when Kaitlin and Corey engaged in this volleyball match, it was a fight to the final point every time. I was proud of how my kids poured themselves into these matches, diving for balls, stretching to return volley, and learning to actually get a serve over the net.

As Kaitlin dove for a shot, her insulin pump fell from her pocket, and her infusion set was ripped from her thigh. This was not good. Although we always carry plenty of extra glucose strips, we rarely take an extra infusion set for a daily outing. We had several infusion sets back at the hotel, but we weren't quite ready to leave the party and Kaitlin didn't want to highlight her unique medical issues in this way. Luckily, she wouldn't require as much insulin as usual because of her high activity level, but she would still need some or her sugar would continue to rise until it became a health threat. It is also very difficult to stabilize her sugar after it gets too far out of whack.

In a sense, this was more of an inconvenience than a crisis since we could always just go back to the hotel room, but that was a few hours away and this was a rare opportunity to see our relatives in western New York. It was then decided that we would perform a little surgery on Kaitlin. Propping her up on the picnic table, we carefully guided the tip of the infusion needle back into the tiny hole in her thigh and then wrapped her leg in duct tape to keep the set in place. We were good for a few more hours at the party and Kaitlin wasn't even embarrassed by all of the attention.

By this time, Kaitlin was about 20 months post-diagnosis and we were becoming very good at improvising when necessary. Not only had we discovered many other ways to fix a torn-out infusion set, but we also developed a sixth sense for finding the drug store when we realized we had forgotten the insulin or glucose strips or pump batteries. Incidentally, those things seemed to only happen to us when we were at least 3 hours from our home! But we've all learned not to panic, not to place blame, and to just take care of the situation.

Kaitlin continued to participate in various sports, out of necessity more than anything else, so it was not surprising when she eventually lost interest. It was important that she maintain physical activity to help control her blood sugar levels, which seemed to creep higher and higher if she was inactive. Luckily, Kaitlin finally found her true love in martial arts, first Shorin Ryu, which originated in the Okinawa Islands of Japan, and later Shoshin Ryu, native to the mainland of Japan. She loves the physical and mental toughness required of the martial arts, describing it as making her *feel powerful.* Of course, I liked the fact that she found an activity that she can not only stick with but also provide her with self defense skills.

Kaitlin's dedication to martial arts is simply amazing. Recently voted student of the month, she insists on practicing with her Sensei (instructor) 4 days per week and she earned her blue belt in half the time it takes most people. After 6 months in Shoshin Ryu, her brother Corey also joined and they have great fun together.

Glucose management is a little easier with martial arts as long as she begins class with a higher-than-normal blood sugar level and pays close attention to the signs and symptoms of hypoglycemia. She gets frustrated when her sugar goes low and she must sit out the session so she continues to improve her management and anticipation of both her sugars and her activity level. Unfortunately, the evening classes frequently lead to lows in the middle of the night and it's very difficult getting up for school after a night dealing with low blood sugars, but all and all, she manages very well and has become quite self-sufficient at handling her medical issues.

9 FINDING SOLACE IN VOLUNTEER WORK

I participated in my first JDRF *Walk to Cure Diabetes* little more than 24 hours after Kaitlin was released from the hospital. I remember crying with every step I took. I raised nearly $2,000 that year, qualifying me for the *Golden Sneaker* award at the annual awards banquet. The following year it was a little more difficult to raise money because Kaitlin's diabetes was well-established and people were a little less generous, but I still raised over $1,500 and qualified for another *Golden Sneaker* award. By the third year, I decided that Kaitlin would be a better advocate for diabetes than me and I was right as people went out of their way to generously donate to my little walker.

I really enjoy volunteering for JDRF, particularly the athletic events, but sometimes the exposure to the realities of juvenile diabetes, with its long-term complications, is just too much for me to bear. This morning I volunteered at a charity event, the *Dirty Half Marathon*, a 13.1-mile trek through the foothills of the Sandia Mountains in Albuquerque, New Mexico, and as is so often the case at JDRF-sponsored events, the race organizers and volunteers, have a personal connection to the disease. Today, the race organizer, who was maybe in his mid-40s, described how he lost his sister about two years ago to complications from a failed kidney-pancreas transplant. I was left with such a sad feeling inside, both for him and his family and also for my daughter because the thought of possibly losing her at such a young age seems so unfair and would deprive the world of one of the brightest, most creative, and kindest people I know.

Sadness comes from a feeling of helplessness, and I often feel helpless to do anything to stop Kaitlin's disease and reverse the damage it has already done. Fortunately, there is always a silver lining and this morning my silver lining was the woman who heads JDRF's New Mexico chapter. All smiles and pregnant with her second child, she described how advancements funded by JDRF make it possible for women like her, with juvenile diabetes, to safely bear children, whereas years ago, doctors would have recommended sterilization. She is truly an inspiration and I appreciate the effort she puts forth at all of these events. I often wish I could be so strong.

Approximately two years following Kaitlin's diagnosis, I stepped up my volunteer activities by becoming a political advocate for JDRF. With my day job not providing me much to feel good about, I found solace in volunteering. It really made me feel good about myself again. Soon after signing up at the Advocacy website, I received a phone call and email inquiring about my availability to meet with Senator Tom Udall. As a former U.S. Representative and former State Attorney General, Tom Udall is well known to New Mexicans and I was understandably excited about the opportunity to not only meet with him but also to lobby for a very important cause.

I was impressed with how wonderfully choreographed the meeting with Sen. Udall was. First, I met his staffers at Tiguex Park in Albuquerque and they coached me and another woman on how the meeting would be conducted and soon afterward, the Senator arrived. Being my first experience as an Advocate, I did not realize that I should have brought my kids along for the photos and to allow Kaitlin to tell her diabetes story, but there would be more opportunities for that sooner than I expected.

The other woman had brought her young son who had been diagnosed with type 1 diabetes as a baby. He was now about 8 years old, skinny as a rail, and very active. This was so good to see, defying many of the hurtful stereotypes that people have regarding diabetes.

So, the little guy told his diabetes story as his mom and I looked on. Later, the other mom recounted episodes where her young son actually lost consciousness due to insulin shock and had to be revived with a glucagon injection. Wow, how lucky we were that we never had such a scare!

As we walked down the paved trail with the Senator and his wife Jill, the staffers snapped several publicity photos as I explained the significance of the *Special Diabetes Program* to people like my daughter, the research that it funded, and our hopes for a cure some day. I found the Senator to be very down to earth and I liked his wife who seemed quite impressed with my knowledge of diabetes and the bills that affect diabetics. Of course, what is there to be impressed about? When your kid has a chronic disease, you as a parent are going to learn everything you can about it.

Within 2 months I received another phone call from JDRF's regional coordinator out of Arizona and this time, she asked if I could go talk to Representative Martin Heinrich, a newly-elected congressman in my district. Understanding how these things worked now, I brought both of my children, Kaitlin and Corey, which made for an extra special meeting and photo opportunity.

We were accompanied by another woman and her son who was now a freshman in college. He had been diagnosed about 10 years earlier and they were experienced Advocates. Rep. Heinrich's knowledge of type 1 diabetes and the research co-sponsored by JDRF was quite impressive. It was evident that the junior congressman had done his homework prior to our visit. He had kids himself and I could see that he genuinely sympathized with the two mothers on the other side of the table, recounting our troubles dealing with our kids' disease. Again, as with my visit with Senator Udall, I felt very good when I left the Congressman's Albuquerque office.

But before I could get much of a break, it was time for *Diabetes Day at the Roundhouse* in Santa Fe. Not one to turn down a request, I gladly volunteered to spend the day hosting the JDRF information booth, answering questions, distributing pamphlets, and meeting one-on-one with New Mexico's politicians, including Representative John Smith, Senator Sue Wilson Beffort, and several unnamed staffers. I was proud of what I was doing. It had meaning. And I found a community where I was understood and accepted.

When Kaitlin was first diagnosed with diabetes, I was always sure to make the distinction that she had *type 1* and not *type 2*. I was also much more supportive of the Juvenile Diabetes Research Foundation than the American Diabetes Association because I felt that the ADA was more dedicated to type 2 diabetes than type 1. However, I am now embarrassed and ashamed at my earlier behavior. While the two types of diabetes have vastly different etiologies, they are both terrible diseases that need to be obliterated from our world. I continue to support both the ADA and JDRF through my own personal donations as well as external fundraising.

I am especially thankful that the ADA runs a diabetes camp in New Mexico's Manzano Mountains each summer. This was a fantastic opportunity for my daughter to spend a week with other children who are dealing with the same issues. The week-long camp keeps them physically active, culturally inspired, and socially accepted. My only regret is that Kaitlin could only attend twice because she no longer qualified after she turned 14. An increasing population of diabetic children and limited space force a cut-off age of 13. But we are hoping that when she is old enough, she will return as a counselor so she can raise the spirits of some newly-diagnosed young diabetic who might just need a big sister to lean on.

Volunteering for these organizations makes me feel good about myself. I do it for myself as much as I do it for Kaitlin and the many others who are dealing with this disease. I remember what it was like during my first JDRF Walk to Cure Diabetes and I continue to be supportive of parents who are having difficulties coping. Most often parents ask me about sleepovers because night-time truly is a scary-time for these parents, but we have to let our children live normal lives. We cannot always be there. One of my greatest accomplishments as a parent is that I have taught my children independence and I know that when the time comes, Kaitlin will be okay on her own and I will have to let her go.

10 PICKING UP THE PIECES

After things went downhill for me at my job, I continued to work there for nearly 2 more years, which was a *big* mistake because of the toll it took on me emotionally and physically. While I continued to do some very good things outside of work, like my volunteer and advocacy work, I felt like an outcast at the office and I eventually retreated into my own little world where I interacted with very few people and tried my best to remain invisible. By my very nature, I am a very hard worker and a people-person, so this was very difficult to handle. Thus, I decided that the courageous thing to do, really the only thing to do, was to quit my six-figure job and go out on my own for better or worse. If I worked hard and pursued my passion, I truly believed I could *make it* on my own.

However, I knew that if I was ever going to make it, I needed some semblance of a plan so one day I actually made a list of things I liked and things I didn't like, not just at work, but in life in general. As I reviewed this list which had grown to over two pages, I realized I didn't even like most of the activities that now dominated my job. So, not only was I under emotional duress in this job, but I didn't even enjoy the work I was doing.

Disillusioned over a job that was poorly-matched to my education, career background, and interests, I reflected back on my life and what I seemed to truly enjoy. Everything pointed back to the one consistent, familiar, and comfortable element in my life, which was sports and fitness. I decided that if I could not exercise, train, or participate in sports anymore (due to my lower back injury), I would at least help others achieve their fitness goals. I already knew more than the average trainer from my preparation for mountain bike racing, marathons, and competitive sports, including soccer, tennis, and skiing.

With no formal education as a personal trainer, I decided to take a personal trainer class at the University of New Mexico and become certified. This was very good for me. I enjoyed the anatomy and physiology, nutrition, kinesiology, and the practical application of what we learned in lecture, and my self-esteem began to rise like mercury in a thermometer. I no longer cared what happened at work because I was doing something for myself, building something that I was proud of.

Next, I contacted a local fitness club and inquired about an internship. At that point, I realized it was time to make a decision—was I really going to do this or not? So, over the one-week Christmas shutdown that our company has each year, I pondered what was best for me and my family. Realizing that money was not everything and that if I was not happy, it would affect the rest of my family, I decided to quit my job. I really needed to attract positive elements into my life and repel the negative, and unfortunately, no matter what I did at work, it would always be negative.

I read *The Secret*, a book by Rhonda Byrne, and started practicing drawing positive energy toward myself and gradually good things started happening. I could feel the cloud hanging over my head begin to dissipate, and so, with very little fanfare, I quietly disappeared from my six-figure job to begin an unpaid internship at a gym with a couple of guys young enough to be my sons.

In addition to training clients at the club, I studied at home for the personal trainer certifications offered by the American Council on Exercise and the National Academy of Sports Medicine. This was a very good move as I learned more about postural assessments and gained a better understanding of kinetic chain function. I finally began to understand my lower back problem and was beginning to get it under control. No doubt leaving my stressful job also contributed to my physical healing as well.

As I write this now, just shy of 3 years since that fateful day in October when I answered my cell phone only to hear that my daughter was on her way to the hospital in an ambulance, I feel nearly healed both emotionally and physically. I am once again out on my road and mountain bikes and I am astounded by my strength—it's true what they say, you never forget how to ride a bike!

Emotionally, I am so much better than I was. I am sorry that my daughter has diabetes. I'm sorry that anyone has diabetes, but I'm glad that she is alive and living a semi-normal life now. Sure, there are things she will never be able to do and she will need to be under the care of a physician the rest of her life, but there are people in this world who are much worse off than us.

I am still trying to figure out how I'd like to spend the rest of my life, but I have learned that you should do what you love and love what you do because you're going to have to do it for a very long time. I am much more content now that I have time to write my daily blogs and short stories, help people become fitter and healthier, and spend more time with my children before they head off to college in a few years. I continue to volunteer for ADA and JDRF and I am active in my kids' schools and with their athletic endeavors.

I thought it was quite fitting that shortly before I quit my job, I read an article in the *Economist* titled "Life begins at 46" and I thought, "Wow, this is great" because I'm 46. However, after I read the article I discovered why life begins at 46—it is because 46 is the nadir of your life. Yes, it is the global mean average age of the lowest, most depressing point in a person's life. On the bright side, things could only get better. And yes, things have gotten much, much better for me.

AFTERWARD

As I write this, Kaitlin is approaching the third anniversary of her diagnosis. I have set aside my writing for so long that it's a difficult to remember the details of the last couple years so I must effectively end the story here. However, the story does not really end here because diabetes is something she will have to live with the rest of her life. I will always worry at night time. I will always worry when she is playing sports. And I will probably be a nervous wreck when she heads off to college in a few more years.

Last year Kaitlin published her first book, *Dimension Jumpers*, a full-length science fiction novel based on string theory about two kids who are trained by mad scientists to carry out research in other worlds. The book can now be found in all of the schools in the Moriarty-Edgewood Public School District and she has received many accolades within our community. Incredibly, she is putting the finishing touches on the sequel which she promises will be more exciting that the first!

I am really blessed with two incredible children—Kaitlin, the budding author and scholar of Japanese language and culture, and Corey, a true Renaissance man, a math and computer whiz who plays three instruments, guitar, bass, and drums, and writes his own music. And what I admire most about them is that they are best friends. As I sit here pecking away at my keyboard, I can hear Corey demonstrating a new drum beat for Kaitlin, and I know it won't be long and they will take a break from their erudite activities to have some fun on the Xbox.

In the 3 years since my daughter's diagnosis, I have seen great acts of love and courage, as well as acts of discrimination and cruelty. But after a rough couple of years, I am finally on a path that gives my life meaning and makes me proud of who I am. I am fortunate that my daughter has always been on that path, both before and after her diagnosis, but for me there was a spiritual metamorphosis that took place, and I think in many ways, I am a much better person than before she was diagnosed.

ABOUT THE AUTHOR

Lori Dotson is a freelance writer living in Edgewood, New Mexico, with her husband and two teenage children. She is President and Founder of DotsoFit, LLC, which is devoted to training, educating and motivating people to achieve their personal best in all of their athletic pursuits. She holds a BA Degree from the State University of New York at Buffalo and an MS Degree from the New Mexico Institute of Mining and Technology and is certified by the National Academy of Sports Medicine and the American Council on Exercise as a personal trainer.